Pen and Ink drawing of Waterside House, 1978.

INTRODUCTION

Smarden village is very special to me — a gem of the past — almost unscarred, unlike so many villages of today. I was born here. My childhood days were filled with powerful memories revolving around spring, summer, autumn and winter, in a little world of their own, hidden from the nearest highway or railway station and surrounded on all sides by orchards and hopgardens.

When I left home at eighteen I soon discovered how small my world had been compared with the big wide one outside waiting to be tasted and absorbed. But somehow, no matter where I have been, I always come back to Smarden and there it is — just as I left it — nothing changed. Riding my bicycle down the street I stop and discuss the weather with a childhood friend or enquire about the next jumble sale, and it feels as if no time had passed at all.

I often wonder what Smarden was like before the motor car arrived, when it really was a world of its own, and when a trip to Ashford, our nearest market town nine miles away, was an occasional lengthy excursion only possible when weather permitted. Life in those days revolved around the seasons and the weather. There must have been much more of a community spirit with the same few families having lived in the village for generations, working the land and all pulling together. Today, if we look in the Parish Register, we can still find the old Smarden names: Batt, Buss, Cooper, Cornes, Gurr, Judge, Morris, Offen and Ottaway. But these old names are slowly dispersing. It is more and more difficult to keep up the old homes that have been in the family for generations and many people end up living in modern bungalows and council estates while commuters to London buy up the old houses and furnish with wall to wall carpeting and video sets.

Coach tours from London bring little old ladies in flowery hats and cardigans out to the orchards in the spring. Amateur photographers and camera clubs expose thousands of rolls of film on our Tudor houses and Norman church. Feature articles on "Picturesque Smarden" appear in British and American magazines and in Dutch and German ones too. Even the BBC and Hollywood has found us, bringing their gum-chewing crews, props and make-up girls to produce historical films in our ancient setting.

But this is all part of life and everything must change. Luckily, for most of the year Smarden is left alone, belonging to those who live in it and who try to keep it genuine and unspoiled.

This book is dedicated to all the people of Smarden, past and present, who have worked so hard to preserve our heritage.

Jenni Rodger.

Smarden in 1925 showing "The Street" still unpaved.

EARLY HISTORY OF SMARDEN

How did our village begin?

Smarden lies in the middle south of the Weald of Kent which was once a huge, impenetrable forest but is now a wide band of undulating farmland — a bright patchwork of well cultivated fields and orchards, hedges and copses and trim villages with mixed farming, fruit orchards and hops.

The great forest was known as Andredsweald — sometimes called the "Jutish Forest". One theory is that the name Smarden is derived from "Hosmarden", the clearing where "Hosmar" and "Osmar" kept their swine. Until recently there were still Hosmars living in Smarden. Another theory is that Smarden is a Saxon name. Den means a clearing in the forest and "smeoru" fat or grease. Farmers living on high ground sent their herds of pigs down each winter to feed off acorns. The swineherds built huts in the dens and each clearing took the name of the family living there. The Rev. Haslewood in his book on Smarden published in 1866 says Smarden is a Saxon word signifiying "a fat valley".

The first mention of Smarden is in the "Mark's Domesday", drawn up towards the end of the eleventh century, as paying a yearly tribute to Canterbury of 7d. It is not mentioned in the Domesday Book proper and there are no records before 1100.

The forest had not always been deserted. Long before the Jutes came it was hunted and traversed by men of the Iron Age where they smelted iron ore with charcoal from local timber. This was developed by the Romans who built roads to serve it besides maintaining and improving the earlier tracks. Charcoal "hearths" twenty feet across have been found in Smarden Woods, and what is possibly a Roman road.

The Wealden charcoal burners were nomadic craftsmen. Iron, lead and glass works used vast quantities of charcoal and the burners moved around the countryside setting up their camps and building their "pets" or "clamps" wherever they were needed. Because of charcoal burning, the woods were clearing rapidly. Now there were pockets of settlements on open and fertile ground divided by wooded areas. As the settlements expanded, so the boundaries became defined and at the close of the eleventh century, settlements had spread to every part of the forest. The lord of the manor encouraged settlement, hoping to make a profit from his dens.

The dens became a regular source of firewood and timber for the uplands. As the population increased, markets were formed and larger and more ambitious buildings were required, needing even more timber for roofing and framing. Felling began to outstrip renewal and the number of settlers increased, not only by new arrivals from the uplands but by the increase of their families.

By the time of the Domesday Book, the clearance and settlement was virtually accomplished and spreading. By the close of the eleventh century, settlements had spread to every part of the Weald and the institutions of a settled countryside had been made — "hundred, parish, manor

Old Postcard of Smarden Village taken in the early 1930s. The Street has now been paved. On the left is the water pump which was used as the village water supply for many years. (Betty Marshall)

and village". In the Parish records occurs the personal occupation name "John Denebra" — an indication of there once being a "denebra" or "fenced-off" pasture in Smarden. The site must have been as Edward Hasted described it in his day, 1798.

"The Parish of Smarden is about four miles across, it lies at a small distance southward of the quarry hills, within the Weald, in a flat low situation, very unpleasant and watery, the soil being a deep miry clay. The eastern parts of it are mostly covered with large coppice woods and the whole of it, from the flatness of it, the wide hedge-rows and quantity of oak trees spread over it, has a very gloomy appearance."

Winter scene by the River Beult.

Smarden Church surrounded by flood waters of the River Beult. The Beult flows through Smarden and is the union of four rainwater courses from the parishes of Great Chart, Shadoxhurst, Halden, Bethersden, Biddenden and Pluckley running into Smarden. Flooding is common and annual (see page 41). This picture of the Church was taken in 1920.

1331 was a year of great significance to Smarden. The Pell family arrived from the Netherlands. They were given land here by King Edward III when he brought a number of Flemish craftsmen to England to manufacture broadcloth. The Pell family lived in the Dragon House in the centre of the village and the shed at the back is where the Smarden weaving industry is said to have begun. Prosperity came to the village and the thriving trade in broadcloth continued almost to the time of the industrial revolution. Our great church was built at this time on the site of an older one, and there was a great boom in house building.

Wool was spun by the villagers — particularly by unmarried women — hence the term "spinster" — and sent to the Pells in the Dragon House to weave and finish. Few villagers had their own looms or engaged in more specialised aspects of cloth production. The woven cloth was then stored in The Cloth Hall, originally known as Church Gate Farm. The Cloth Hall acted as a warehouse, storing and cleaning the finished cloths.

At this time village life was centred around the church. The nave was frequently used for all kinds of secular purposes — markets, meetings, rallying in times of danger, and sometimes even a shelter for sheep and swine. It was also used as a warehouse for the goods of merchants. The doorways were "large enough for layden packhorses". The church was sometimes called "the granary of the Weald" and people took refuge there from floods, with their grain and animals.

The population of Smarden in the Elizabethan period was comparable to that of today, about 1,000. The parish covered twenty-five square miles in 1575 and today it covers thirty square miles. In 1450 there were four clothmakers, six butchers, four carpenters, five tailors, eight weavers and twelve husbandmen. In a census taken in 1800, the population increased from 831 to 1,130 and in 1861 there were 214 inhabited buildings and 7 uninhabited.

MAP – PLAN OF SMARDEN TOWN AND NAMES OF RESIDENTS IN 1783

Arrived at by collating the Tithe Map of 1838 with Richard Large's plan, August, 1783.

- Stile beside the "Brothers' House"
- Minnis Stile
- Isaac Bott
- Road to Pluckley
- Mr Hogben, Gent
- Thos. Vannal, Watch Maker
- Thos. Fagg, Cordwainer
- Butcher Hooker's House
- Town Barn
- Cow Lodge
- Smith's shop
- Stable and Horse pond
- Henry Harnden, Weaver
- Mrs. Jell
- Gilletts
- A weaver's shed
- Butcher Hooker's shop
- Gate House
- Geo. Gooding, Barber
- (Dadson's) School House
- Elizans. Pell.
- House belonging to W. Fry
- Wm. Ottaway, Carpenter
- Blacksmith's shop
- Shop kept by Stephen Chittenden
- Chequers kept by W. Evenden
- Road to Bethersden
- Empty
- Sign of the White Horse kept by John Wilmot
- Shop kept by J. Judge
- The Poor Row
- Church yard
- Shoesmith
- Doctor's Row
- Nubs Green
- Mr Jas. Ottaway, farmer
- Road to Headcorn
- Mr Thos. Dawson, Tailor
- My Lodgings (R. Large 1783)
- Mr Hinds, A rich farmer

H.L.M. 1.iii.1925

This map was first drawn by Richard Large in 1783 and used as a Tithe Map of the village up to and after the year 1838.

This map of Smarden was drawn by Jim Sparks for the Charter Fair of 1972, and shows sketches of the most interesting houses of the village. More than 100 of the houses and buildings in Smarden are officially listed as being of architectural or historic interest. In the restoration of Williamsburg in Virginia, U.S.A., Smarden is mentioned as one of the English villages from which much of the architecture of the 18th-century American capital was derived.

Hartnup House today. It is thought that Mathew Hartnup arranged for the building of our row of cottages around the corner on Water Lane for they have always been known as "Doctor's Cottages" and were used for the sick and the elderly needing treatment.

Schools

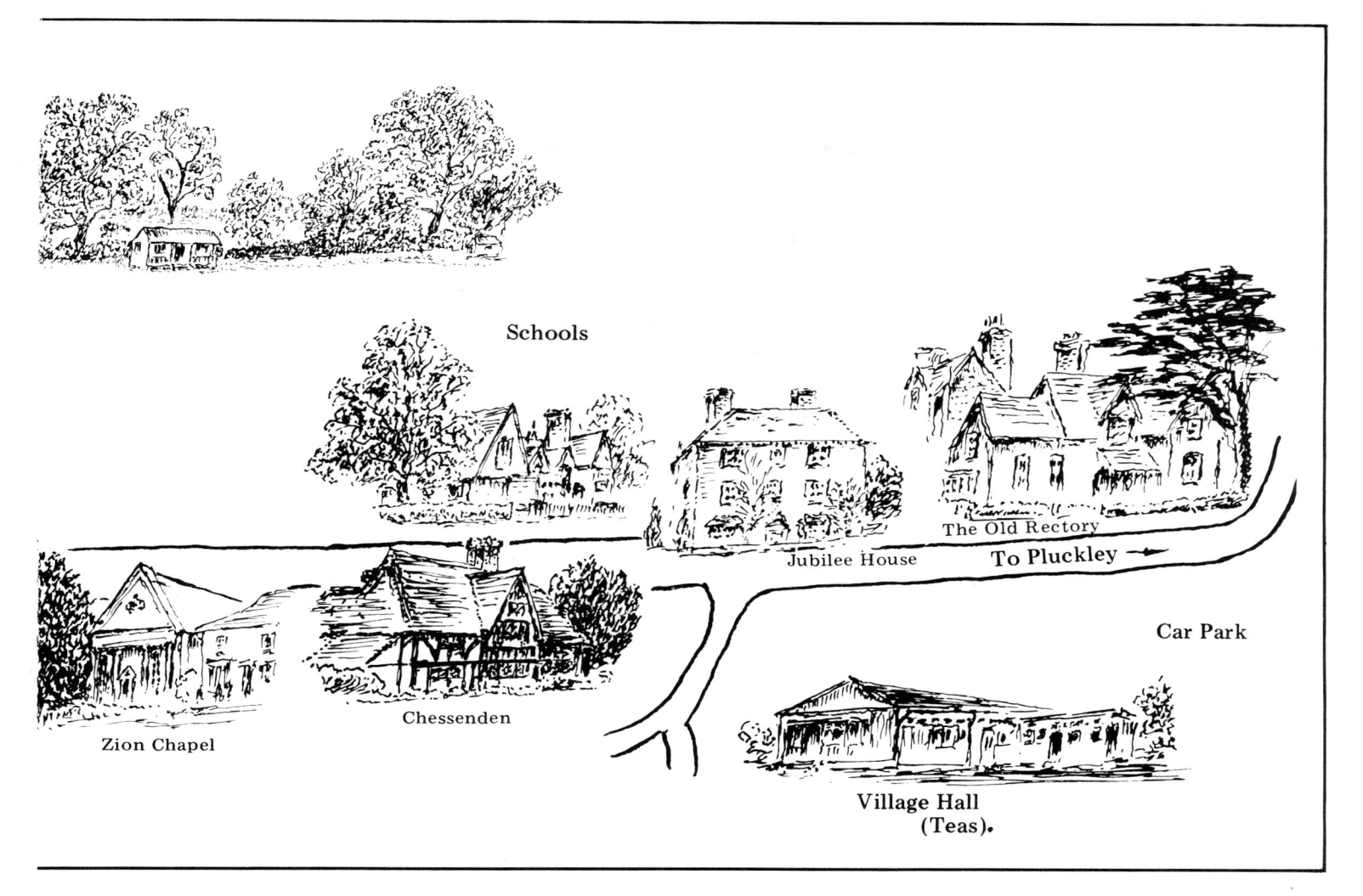

Jubilee House
The Old Rectory
To Pluckley

Car Park

Zion Chapel
Chessenden
Village Hall (Teas).

Ben Springett who owned the Smarden bicycle shop and lived at Hartnup House in 1910.

Hartnup House in 1866.

HARTNUP HOUSE

In spite of its prosperity, Smarden had a large proportion of poor people and was by law responsible for looking after them. "Poor houses" were maintained and managed by Overseers of the Poor and from their accounts much can be learned of social conditions in the village. Doctors, then known as apothecaries, began to practise professionally, the most famous being Mathew Hartnup, a Baptist and Physician, who came to Smarden during the 17th Century.

In 1671 he extended his house and carved on the fascia a "rhinoceros" emblem of the Apothecaries, the company to which he belonged. On the beam carvings, one can see both York and Lancaster roses and Mathew Hartnup's name.

The "rhinoceros" emblem of the Apothecaries carved in the oak beam below the gable.

Waterside House before renovation.

WATERSIDE HOUSE

When my parents bought "Doctor's Cottages" in 1958, they were four small half-timbered cottages built in late Tudor times, sitting in a row under one roof of old Kentish hand-made peg tiles. Before becoming one house, we had 16 tiny rooms, four staircases and 36 doorways, not one of which was more than 5 feet 8 inches high. During the 350 years that our cottages have stood on Water Lane they must have changed hands many times and indeed local villagers have told me proudly that they had been born in one of our cottages.

My father spent two years looking for old hand-made bricks and tiles and centuries old oak timbers, taking me with him in his Landrover as he toured Kent in search of genuine old building materials. We lived first in one cottage, and then as the work progressed spread to the next. Then my two brothers were born and we added on here and there. The actual building took more than seven years.

With the help of a handy local builder, Bob Ponsford, my father slowly converted "Doctor's Cottages" into one house, adding more rooms as the family increased. It took seven years actual building but of course a house is never finished. Here Bob is tiling the bay window which looks out over Water Lane.

The Bell Inn: a group outside the Bell Inn before 1890. Left to right: The Bell blacksmith Jim Wood, unknown, unknown, William Offen, Landlord. Sitting, L to R: George Day, Thomas Offen, unknown.
(Mrs. Ernest Offen)

SMARDEN PUBS

Smarden boasts three historic pubs — The Chequers, the Flying Horse and the Bell.

Just around a steep corner from our house at the top of The Street is the Chequers Inn, once a popular resort for smugglers. Local legend says there is a tunnel under the Chequers leading to the church. When the road was torn up recently to install a new drainage system we had a good look for the remains of a tunnel — but it must have caved in many years ago. Local legend also says there was once a double chimney in The Chequers where casks of brandy were hidden, and everyone knows that one of the small front bedrooms is HAUNTED. Smugglers changed horses here on their way to the coast and their mounts were shod at the forge next door.

The Chequers was bought at the end of the 17th Century along with its malt house and three acres of land for 120 guineas. In 1888 the pub changed hands and the same property sold for 900 guineas. There are dozens of pubs in Kent called "The Chequers" but ours is the only one with rounded weather boarding which stretches around the corner into Water Lane.

Several quotes from the past remind me of what the Chequers Inn meant to the local residents:

"Gypsies would come and sit in a circle in the bar singing, us all crowding the door to listen."

"I spent all day in the Chequers playing the accordion and singing while the horse was shod."

"I first heard 'The Man Who Broke the Bank at Monte Carlo' at The Chequers."

"Smarden women were never seen in the pubs — Pluckley women, yes."

The Flying Horse is located behind the church on Cage Lane. This photograph shows Tom White, aged 2, with his mother Mrs. Charles White outside "The Flyer" in 1880. Charles White was then the licensee. When he died, Charles Marshall took over the Inn and the Marshall family ran it for many years. (Betty Marshall, grand-daughter of the former licensee, remembers customers coming in for a beer and sitting all evening listening to the piano. The more energetic played darts and "shove ha'pennies". "But it was all put away on a Sunday".)

The oldest pub is the Bell Inn, said to be continuously in operation since 1400. Rupert Croft-Cooke, in his book "The Happy Highways", described the Bell Inn as it was half a century ago.

"Two hundred yards down the road was a pub called the Bell. It seemed to me then, and seems now in recollection, to have all that I most value in the tradition of the English inn. It was an old timbered building but its antiquity was not speciously preserved or stressed, its public rooms were not cluttered with antiques, it was not quaint or old-world but a sensibly furnished, cheerful, well-kept tavern in which for three centuries liquor had been sold without fuss or folksiness to the local farmers, their men and a few passing travellers".

At the start of the Second World War, Mrs. Gorden Hughes, wife of the Landlord of the Bell, described what happened there the day war was declared.

"... with the sounding of the very first air raid warning the hop pickers left their drinks and ran helter skelter back to their families. This annoyed old Sam Austen who stood in the doorway cursing first the hop pickers and later the Germans, saying that for nearly sixty years he had been coming to The Bell and no German was ever going to stop him! Gas masks were issued. About this time the Battle of Britain started and each day above our heads planes zooming and fighting left vapour trails in the sky. Each day brought air raids with hundreds of bombers above us on their way to London, looking like little silver gnats, while the very air seemed to throb with the roar of engines".

The Flying Horse (Percy Small)

The Chequers Inn in 1956. (Thomas Bushell)

During World War II soldiers were quartered in The Cloth Hall. Captain John Noel of Everest fame (he was on the 1924 Mallory expedition to Mount Everest) restored the house to its present state soon after the War. This picture shows The Cloth Hall before restoration when it was known as Turk Farm. In front is an old snow plough.

THE CLOTH HALL

Imagine you are approaching the village from the west along a country lane. There are hedges on either side and beyond stretch orchards and pastures and fields with sheep and cows. You pass hop gardens and a few oast houses with tall white cowls and old half-timbered or red brick farmhouses, many with great wooden barns. You may have crossed the River Beult at Hadman's Bridge, parts of which are of medieval structure.

Before World War II, a magnificent avenue of oak trees lined the road as you near the village. These were cut down to build a long line of Council Houses, known ironically as "The Oaks."

On your right you will see a fine example of a typical Wealden Hall House. It was built in about 1420 and was originally the farmhouse belonging to the church. After the Dissolution of the Monasteries it came into the possession of a cloth merchant, Tomas Yates. He fitted it up as his residence and warehouse for wool woven in the village. A pulley for hoisting the bales of wool to the storerooms can be seen on the north side. With a steep-tiled roof, walls of timber and plaster, out houses and a great wooden barn, it has been called a perfect specimen of a yeoman's 15th Century timber house.

The Cloth Hall, date of completion 1450, is known as Churchgate Farm on ordnance maps, in old documents as Park Farm and more recently as Turk Farm. The ancient and well-carved ceiling and staircase prove that the house throughout must have been fitted up in costly style, evidently for a rich man.

The north-west end of The Cloth Hall shows the original timbers three floors up to the wool hoist. Opposite is a typical Wealden oast house, its cowls restored and in perfect condition.

The Cloth Hall, then known as Turk Farm, before being restored in the 1940s.

Smarden village forge before 1914. Old Mr. Fred Ripley, blacksmith for many years, stands on the right beside the wheel platform on which is an upturned shim. His sons did not work regularly at the forge and the assistant standing on the left is not thought to be one of them.

Smarden Street today. We often have the Morris Dancers coming here to practice and perform. They like our legendary background and enthusiastic on-lookers.

THE STREET

Smarden Street is lined on either side by half-timbered or white weather-boarded houses with red-tile roofs. On the right is the village post office, almost unchanged for the past fifty years. Fading photographs show what The Street looked like in the old days.

The old roads to and from Smarden were soft and often impassable and in the winter paved causeways, made of Bethersden marble slabs, were laid along them. Among these slippery, uncemented stones pack horses and men toiled for many years. The causeways never crossed a parish boundary and all led to the Church, following an order from King John that everyone must attend Church. Few of the Bethersden marble slabs are left today, being a great temptation to road menders, farmers and garden path menders.

Many of our roads were still "soft" in 1900. Henry Brazier, still living in 1925, said that he remembered, as a wagoner, carrying women from his wagon to the shops in Smarden, and to their houses, and that this was the custom. Others remember standing up to their hips in ruts at Walford House not far from the Church to watch four horses pull out an empty wagon. Sometimes the roads were churned into mud, slub and slime as deep as the wheel feloes so that a wagon's front axle drove the mud before it.

When I was first pushed up the village street in my pram, my mother was able to purchase all her household needs

An old Postcard of The Street looking down from the church. The road was still unpaved and full of ruts. On the left is George Springett's bike shop which replaced the forge. Date: 1910.   (Winnie Buckman)

from local shops. We had a home bakery, a butcher's shop, two large groceries, a cider factory, two garages, a bicycle shop run by "Pop" Marshall, Smarden's friend to everyone on two wheels, and Mr. Wheatley the shoe-maker, a craftsman of the first order. Sadly the village shops closed down, one by one, due to inflation and competition from supermarkets in neighbouring towns. Today we have the same butcher's shop but no bakery. We have one grocer's shop almost a mile from the village green. But we do have three antique shops, very close together, on The Street.

THE PENT HOUSE

View of the Pent House with the church in the background.

No one can go through the church-yard from the village street without passing under what is commonly called the Pent House. This is an old church word and is used for an open shed or projection over a door to form a protection against the weather. It was not without its use. The room over it is a modern addition. The ancient part of this shed was the old Lych-gate. The word "Lych" (or "lich") means the roofed gateway of the church where a coffin awaits the arrival of the clergyman.

In olden times the corpse was carried to its burial by the friends and neighbours of the deceased and they had often far to travel. Their time of reaching the church-yard must have been uncertain and this uncertainty no doubt caused delay when they arrived. Therefore it was desirable to have a place of shelter on a rainy day and a rest when the way was long.

Today the Pent House is the name, also, of the attractive house built over it and where I spent a great deal of my early childhood. Peeping from the windows towards the church or towards the Street was always an adventure. Smarden may be a small village but there was always something going on, even if it was just Mrs. Twigg-Mossley on her way to post a letter.

Peeping the other way I had a good view of the church and the TOMBSTONES. These are numerous and ancient and many have unusual inscriptions. One that struck my imagination when I was old enough to wander around and read them haunted me every time the River Beult rose over its banks:

"In memory of Samuel
Son of Richard and Elizabeth Bayly
of this Parish
Who died December the 17th, 1759
Aged 29 years.
He was unfortunately
Drowned in the River
Near Rumden in this Parish."

My father bringing me home from church under the old Lychgate.

Smarden church in the snow.

A postcard of Smarden Church taken in the early 1930s. Picture shows Water Lane entrance to the Church, and on far right, a shed which once was part of Hartnup House. (Betty Marshall)

THE CHURCH OF ST. MICHAEL THE ARCHANGEL

The earliest accounts of Smarden Church are lost in antiquity; we have no record of the pious man who founded it. It is dedicated to St. Michael the Archangel and is popularly known as "The Barn of Kent" on account of its singular construction, being nearly 36 feet wide without side aisles. The roof is unique as there is but one tie-beam.

On a plaque facing the main entrance is an impressive list of all the Rectors of Smarden, dating back to the year 1205 when Adam de Essex was presented to the benefice by King John, and followed over the centuries by sixty-one men of the cloth, including the Rev. Francis Haslewood who wrote "The Antiquities of Smarden" in 1866 and from whose reference to the church I quote:

"He who builds to God and not to fame;
Will never mark the marble with his name."

There is no evidence of what kind of church existed earlier than the 14th century. The main structure of the building we see today was probably built between 1325 and 1350 but the tower dates from the late 15th century.

Our church registers go back to the year 1632. A transcript of an earlier register, starting in 1560 but not complete, is in the library of Canterbury Cathedral.

The church plate includes a Queen Anne silver chalice and paten engraved with the date 1714.

There is a peal of six bells, recast in 1922 from a former peal of five. The oldest bell, bearing the founder's name and the date — Robertus Mot me fecit, 1601 — was re-cast separately in its own metal with those words remoulded. The old inscriptions and dates were repeated on the other bells.

Wednesday night is bell-practice night in Smarden and the heavy clanging of six great bells booming out from the church tower across the road from my bedroom is one of my earliest memories. I cried every Wednesday night from seven to nine o'clock and in turn my brothers cried after me. My mother tolerated bell-ringing night with a determined respect for necessity and tradition but often she would gather all three of us children and take us off in the car for a long drive on a warm summer night. We had to drive a good five miles from Smarden before we were out of ear-shot. On bell-ringing night our 350-year-old house shakes and rumbles and shifts and reverberates. But we have all stopped crying now and have almost learned to enjoy it.

Because of their skill and devotion to weekly practice, Smarden bell ringers are rated amongst the best in Kent.

"Beating the Bounds". This photograph, taken in 1931, shows the then Bishop of Dover being swung by parishioners before the annual Beating of the Bounds ceremony.
(Kentish Express)

Row of Smarden boys lining up to be "beaten" before the annual "Beating the Bounds" ceremony at St. Michael's Church.
(Kentish Express)

Above: interior of Smarden Church. This shows the great width of the nave — 36 feet, with the unusual feature of having no aisles, giving it the name "Barn of Kent". Part of the "scissors-beam" roof can be seen. The altar rails are 17th century. On either side of the chancel is a stone reredos with five arches. These originally contained wall paintings which had perished, so in 1907 modern paintings were put in their place using models of Smarden people. The east (back) window has attractive tracing but the glass is Victorian; the remaining three windows in the nave are mid-15th century.

Below: Richard Nelson-Smith is christened in St. Michael's Church by Canon F. W. Phillips. The font has been repaired and replastered over the years but there is enough detail still visible to date it confidently to the 14th century.

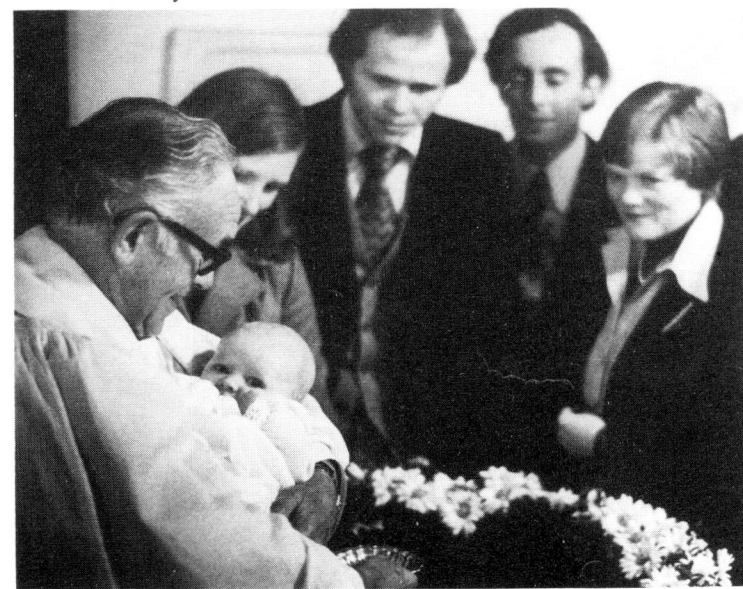

Left: repairing and painting the church clock which over the years keeps perfect time and strikes every quarter of an hour.

Town Bridge, from which we watch the seasons pass.

THE RIVER BEULT AND TOWN BRIDGE

The Beult River, one of the principal feeders of the Medway, flows through Smarden close below the village under a stone bridge of two arches.

> "We are greatly indebted to our river, not that it brings any traffic through Smarden and contributes to our prosperity for we know it is not navigable, but it drains the parish and makes it healthy and fertile, which probably it would not be were it not that the river serves as a main drain".

These words were written by that venerable historian of Smarden, the Rev. Francis Haslewood, 100 years ago. He adds:

> "Although Smarden lies low, it is nevertheless healthy and this is accounted for as some suppose from the fact that the water is strongly impregnated with iron. To prove the healthiness of the parish one has only to turn to the registers to see how many have reached their 'three score years and ten'. There is a tombstone in the churchyard to the memory of Mary Lucas who died in 1724 in the 104th year of her age".

However, old residents of Smarden have particularly asked not to be buried too close to the River when their time came as they had a great fear of their bodies rising up in the flood waters and floating through the churchyard into the Street.

When not in flood, the River Beult is a graceful flowing stream. I once spotted an otter there, and many times a solitary kingfisher as well as numerous heron and Canadian geese.

Town Bridge, previously known as Church Bridge, was built in 1650. An earlier oaken structure and ford causeway preceded it. The Beult, notorious for its flooding, claimed several wagoners' lives in times past.

The "Fleur-de-lys" carving in the Thatched House.

The Thatched House before renovation.

THE THATCHED HOUSE

On the other side of the church, beyond the River Beult, is the Thatched House, once called Elizabeth Cottage or Thorpe House. My best friend lived there when I was a little girl and we played happily in that lovely old world garden and hid under secret stairways.

It was formerly an Elizabethan cottage, definitely a weaver's house, for at each end there were flax chambers on the first floor and one of these is still much as it was then, open to the rafters. The chambers had long doors opening out of the wall so that sheaves of flax could be brought in off the loaded wagons outside to be dried indoors. There were no windows in these rooms.

The moat in front of the house is filled in today but it would have been the "retting" pond. In the principal bedroom there is a panel of carved wood tracery making a "fleur-de-lys" pattern against the white plaster wall, which is thought to have been the work of one of the Flemish craftsmen.

The Thatched House after renovation, in 1959–1961.

The Dragon House.

THE DRAGON HOUSE

The Dragon House was built in 1331 by a family of Flemish weavers and, architecturally, this Wealden house has a familiar Dutch influence with its high-pitched peg-tiled roof. The original structure was extended in the 17th century when the main chimney was added.

The first floor weaving room still has its original loading door and windows visible from the interior. The weaving shed, in which villagers were taught the skill, still stands in the garden. A thirty-foot deep bell well is situated in the front garden. It is constantly full of fresh, drinkable spring water. The nearby Victorian village pump still draws its water from this source.

With its prominent overhanging frontage, the cantilever principle of the dragon beam is used to support the upper storeys. The name derives from the dragon-tail appearance of the ceiling beams which radiate from the two diagonal weight-bearing timbers, each one supported towards its end by the massive carved corner posts. The house name, however, presumably derives from the dragon-like carvings on the exterior. These heraldic Wyverns were apparently a fairly popular adoption by many of the newly-rich weavers, the choice based on a pun of their occupation, weaving.

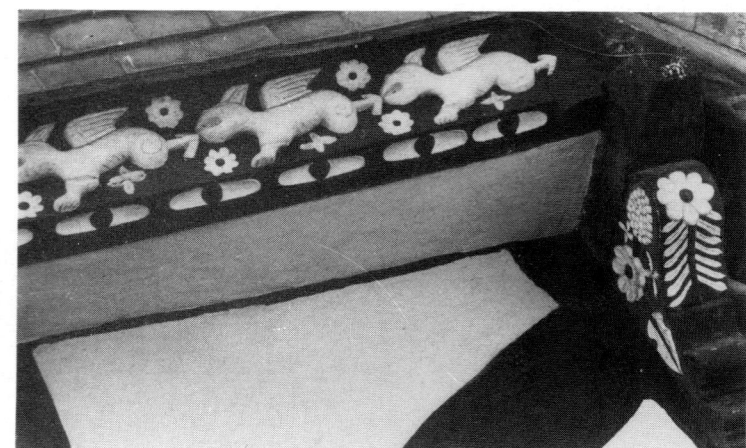

Detail of Dragons carved into the beam over the first-floor window.

Following the reduction in local weaving, the Dragon House was often used as a local shop serving the village community over many years. In a front room cavity discovered during recent alterations, there was found a complete cobbler's display board of Elizabethan shoe styles.

Chessenden in the 1860s, from Haslewood's "Antiquities of Smarden".

CHESSENDEN

Another very beautiful hall house that looks across the Minnis is Chessenden, built in 1462. A big half-timbered house, Chessenden is the best example in Smarden of the typical Wealden arrangement of an open hall between two-storeyed wings, overhanging but kept within the simple hipped roof. First the hall had a floor put across it, then came the two-storeyed canted bay added in 1558 and a gable over it, close studding in the centre, curved braces in the wings and a blocked four-centred doorway.

Known as Smarden House until some 80 years ago, Chessenden was at one time the village banqueting hall as well as the Workhouse.

A solar screen in what was the hall is one of the few surviving in Kent and still in remarkable condition.

Drawing of Chessenden after conversion. The house was converted and modernised soon after World War II.

Smarden School in 1906. The girls in white smocks sat in the front rows, the boys in the back.   (Mrs. E. Ledger and Mrs. Jim Morris)

Smarden schoolchildren in the winter of 1964, on the occasion of the "50th Anniversary of the "new school".

Smarden schoolchildren practicing maypole dancing in the front playground. Maypole dancing is always performed by the children at major village events.

SMARDEN SCHOOL

By the generosity of Stephen Dadson, a bricklayer of Bethersden who could not read or write, a Trust was formed in 1716 for the provision of land and a dwelling house for a "free school" with an annual endowment. The "old schoolhouse" still stands in the village street but the school itself was moved to the other end of the village when the new building was constructed in 1864, the cost being met partly by money from the bequest and partly by contributions from public bodies and private subscriptions. The income from the Dadson Trust is still administered to this day and part of the money is used to give Bibles to each school leaver but the school itself has long been incorporated into the state system.

Smarden School, not the most attractive building in the village, nevertheless is happily situated alongside the Minnis and the children of Smarden spend their formative years in a healthy, happy atmosphere surrounded by acres of green playgrounds.

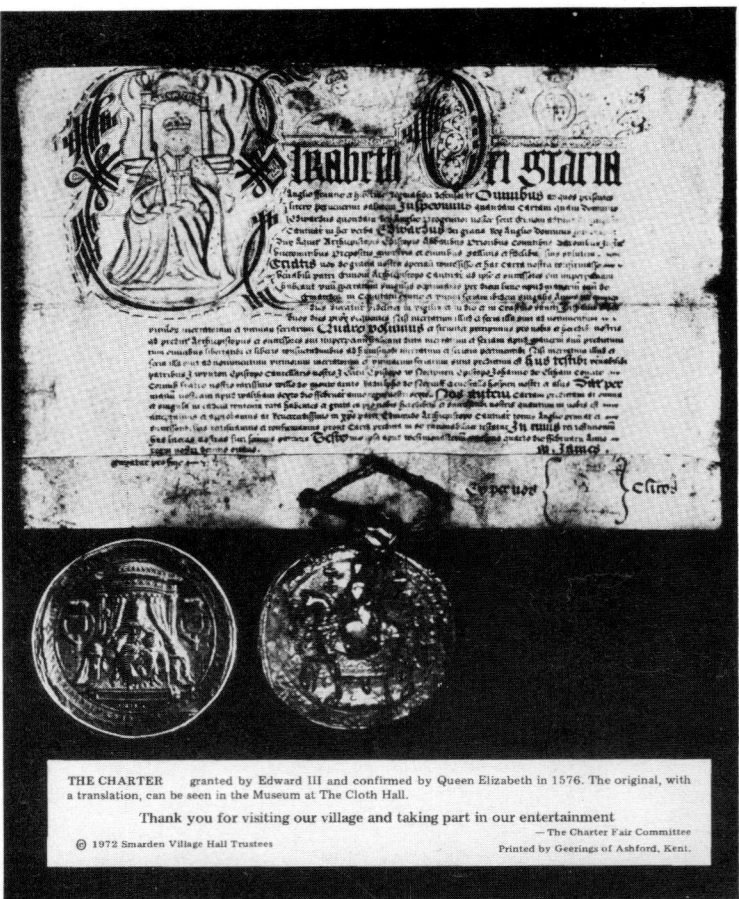

Back cover of Fair Programme, showing reproduction of the Charter granted by Edward III and confirmed by Queen Elizabeth in 1576. The original is now in the Maidstone Museum. (George Rodger)

Jenni and Jonny Rodger ringing the bell to attract customers to the bran tub held in our garden during the Charter Fair of 1964.

CHARTER FAIR

The story begins nearly 700 years ago when King Edward III brought weaver craftsmen over from Flanders to make use of the Kentish wool, ponds and fuller's earth to set up a weaving industry to make broadcloth in our village.

Fourteenth century broadcloth was a dense fabric comprising loosely twisted yarn which required shrinking before it was fit to wear. Smarden's secret lay in the art of "fulling" (cleansing and thickening) after the cloth came from the loom. By using "marl" (a soil consisting of clay and lime making a valuable fertilizer) abundant in the area, the wool was then purified by the use of grease and wooden hammers driven by water power. This produced a smooth even-surfaced broadcloth.

Smarden had unique methods of carding and combing the wool. Carding comes from the Latin "carous" denoting a miller's teasel, a kind of thistle used to smooth and range the nap of the cloth. Dressing the flax was the next stage and required a large pond, known as a Rhode pond, rhode meaning a stack of flax. Smarden had such a pond, situated north-east of the Cloth Hall. The flax was tied in bundles and sunk in the water and dried. This process shrunk the fibres of the flax together so that the tighter, smoother cloth was produced.

Smarden prospered under these new skills and in recognition of its success, King Edward III granted the village a Royal Charter.

In 1572 the church bells rang out to herald the arrival of Queen Elizabeth I. She was en route from Sissinghurst Castle to Boughton Malherbe. Evidently impressed by what she saw in Smarden, in 1576 she officially ratified the Charter granted by Edward III and thus the village acquired the status of a town.

The Elizabethan Charter hangs today in St. Michael's church recognising that Smarden is still worthy of its heritage and grants that, whenever needs arise, the people of Smarden recall their charter and hold an Elizabethan fair.

The original charter, written on parchment, is a fine specimen of penmanship and is still in excellent preservation, as is also the great seal belonging to it. On one side it represents Queen Elizabeth on horseback bearing a sceptre in her left hand. On the other she is on her throne, holding a sceptre in her right hand and an orb in her left. Over her head is a canopy, on either side of which are the royal arms and order of the Garter.

I was five when I experienced my first Charter Fair. I remember my brother Jonny was two and we were dressed in red tights with white smocks and caps. There was a bran tub by the pond and my father hung strings of brightly coloured flags all around the front garden. A lady took us by the hand and led us through crowds of people dressed in funny costumes and the village street was full of music and bustle, Morris dancers and market stalls.

A modern Queen Elizabeth I arrives on her horse to meet her public. Photo taken at The Cloth Hall during the Charter Fair of 1976.

The celebrations began with the pealing of bells in St. Michael's Church. The opening pageant recalled the day Queen Elizabeth I rode through our village on horseback and a present day horsewoman was chosen to lead the parade, side-saddle, on a magnificent white horse. After the presentation of the Charter to the "worthies of Smarden" trading began up and down the street, everyone dressed in Elizabethan costume and the ancient arts and crafts were revived in gaily decorated stalls. There was maypole dancing on the Minnis, Morris dancing on the street, and Kentish farmhouse teas in the school. In the Tudor barn of the Cloth Hall, a unique collection of farm implements, kitchen utensils and various curiosities spanning 500 years of Kentish life were displayed. Various amusements included jousting, Beat the Pig, the Pillow Pole and Mallet and Bell and those who wished could pay for the privilege of sitting in the old Smarden stocks.

I was seventeen when we last held a Charter Fair. It had been a wonderful, sunny day and hundreds of people had come to pay homage to our village. The sun was slowly setting over the corn fields as I made my way homeward, walking back across the village green past coconut shies, jesters and laughing children and then through the village street where Elizabethan music wafted over the people in the market stalls packing up for the day. I knew I would remember all this for a lifetime.

There are still some beautiful oast houses in Smarden which have been converted now into modern dwellings. This double oast is just around the corner from us on Water Lane, opposite the Cloth Hall.

HOPS

Early in the 19th century Smarden was no longer a manufacturing centre and had become what it is today — a country village engaged in agriculture, the farms in the parish being largely middle-sized family units.

In 1831 hops were introduced and became the staple crop under the leadership of Mr. W. Hinds. The hop gardens brought some prosperity to the village until crop restrictions of later years caused the forty or more oasts to fall into disuse and by 1917 only 37 acres were under cultivation. Many of the hop gardens were subsequently planted with apple trees which do well in our heavy clay soil.

Hop picking used to draw many outside labourers. 50,000 hop-pickers once came to Kent from the East End of London each September and camped by the hundreds beside the hedgerows as the hops ripened. The army of harvest hands worked through the fields like locusts. Cutters attacked the vines, strippers standing beside their bins pulled off the clustered hops.

Now machines have taken over. Vines trundle in the bins behind tractors. Mechanical fingers pluck them clean. On mechanised farms today one may find twelve men doing a job that formerly would have occupied several hundred.

In 1962 Mabel Buckman wrote about the old days in the Kent hop gardens for the West Kent W.I. news.

"Hop picking seems to have been with me all my life. My father had a mixed farm, Biddenden Green Farm, Smarden, and hops played an important part in the year's

Veteran hop driers John and Isaac Judge pose with a sack of A. Birt Hops. The Birts lived on Cage Lane near the Thatched House but their hop gardens have long since disappeared.

William, son of Walter Morley with his fiancée Dorothy Smith outside the Mill, 1904. The tandem belonged to Fred Buss who would bike to Smarden from the top of Sutton Valence Hill with his wife in the chair.

work. Father did his own hop drying, my brother measured and at ten years of age I took on the booking. We had twelve bins and all home pickers, mostly neighbours and friends. We measured four times a day, the green hops being measured into bags called 'Pokes', made of a loose woven string in a shade of green. Ten bushels were put into each poke and a farm wagon collected and took them to the oast house. Hops were grown on poles about ten or twelve feet high and these were pulled out of the ground and laid by the bins. Sometimes we stripped a pole and placed it across the horns of the bin, then rested the pole of hops on it for easier picking. This was called a 'horse-pole'.

We had a month's picking and by the end of September the mornings were decidedly cool. I remember my brother gathering loose wood and broken hop poles and making a bonfire and children soon gathered round enjoying the warmth. About 9.30 a.m. we were ready for a snack, having had breakfast at 6 a.m. Mother was famous for her pastries of meat, cheese, jam and sugar cakes and we soon made short work of them. She used to bake twice a week in the evening. We had a bricked oven heated with faggots and I can see her now, sweeping out the red embers".

This shows West End Mill in the late 1880s with various members and friends of the Cornes family posed formally around the pond, in the garden, and on the steps to the mill itself.

SMARDEN MILLS

West End Mill, south of the church, also called "Town Mill" or "Corne's Mill" was originally built in the 12th century, probably at the same time as our church. It belonged to the Cornes family for many years and was still working in 1912. It was a post mill (or "stump" mill) and had four sweeps covered with canvas. The mill provided generations of Smardonians with whole meal bread and stone ground flour, not to mention poultry spice, flint grit and oyster shell. When Thomas Cornes inherited the mill from his father early this century he advertised widely by way of lavish calendars his "Wedding and Birthday Cakes Made to Order."

Sadly the mill fell down in 1954 and has never been rebuilt. Old photographs capture its original glory.

Wreckage of West End Mill when it collapsed in 1954.

Wreckage of West End Mill, showing the oak of the wheel, with hornbeam teeth and metal spokes. (A. Vallens)

East Mill or Black Mill. This was a smock mill dating back to 1804. It was last worked in 1923, after which it rapidly fell into disrepair.

There are many lovely old barns in Smarden, and no doubt these will one day be turned into attractive residences by country-loving commuters.

Sheep and apple orchards surround Smarden Village.

COUNTRY LIFE

Smarden today still has a farming community. There are about eighteen farms of under 40 acres, twenty-five of 40–100 acres, 14 of over 100 acres and one farm of over 200 acres. Cattle form the mainstay of the farming industry; there are very few dairy farms. Beef cattle are reared and cows and bullocks are a familiar sight, as are sheep. But the land is heavy and full of clay and only 25% of Smarden's acreage is arable. Many of the former hop gardens were subsequently planted with apple trees which do well in the heavy soil and cider-making has become almost our only industry. Each autumn the potent scent of rotting apples drifts over the village as great lorry-loads are dumped at the cider factory behind Water Lane.

The Church and Cage Lane in the early 1900s. In the foreground is Mr. H. Martin, the schoolmaster, and his dog, "Nipper".
(Mr. E. Ledger)

In 1912 the haying was done with wooden rakes on Shirley Batt's farm near Romden Castle.

James Buckman, farmer, and his daughter Grace who lived at Biddenden Green Farm. Photo taken c. 1919.

Going away. The wedding of Mr. John Pearson and Miss Dora Small in 1910. Taken outside East End House (formerly Grant's Village Grocery Shop). Mr. and Mrs. John Pearson are in the back seat.

George Buckman, son of James, who took over the farm.

Mr. Albert Small on his milk round in 1906. (Percy Small)

Outside the Pearson's Draper's shop in 1907. From left to right: John Brown, Ernest Pearson, Edgar King, John Pearson, Tom Rutherford. Pearson's shop eventually became Grant's Grocery Shop which survived until the early 1970s.

VILLAGE LIFE

Smarden is a village with a strange hold on the affections of those who have known it. Old folks of the village look back to when they were young and regret many of the modern changes. When the old barn in the middle of the village burned down, they were sad as it had been for many years the carpenter's shop of the Gurr family, and the blacksmith's forge opposite has completely vanished. The cottage beside it where Fred Ripley the Blacksmith lived is now in ruins. West End Mill collapsed with age. The beautiful oak trees which stood north of the church from Water Lane on the way to Headcorn have been cut down to make way for council houses and these also occupy the glebe of the Old Rectory, Beult Meadow and Chessenden Lane. Once the scene of Sunday School treats, Green Lane is now replaced by modern bungalows. Still, most of the new buildings are tucked pretty well out of sight and as you walk down the Street today you may wonder whether you really are in the 20th Century as the village magically remains almost unchanged from its former old world charm.

Smarden is still a close community, having no main road adjoining it and no railway station. Newcomers are still called "foreigners" but it has become a welcoming joke. A

Mr. and Mrs. Law who lived in Churchgate Cottage in the early part of this century. She sold home-made sweets.

Mr. Wells the tailor who also made coats for the Turner Charity. These were dark brown with a cape and were given to six old Smarden men annually. (Miss Jane Morris)

Old Mrs. Buckman who used to live in Cage Cottages and attended Zion Chapel (date: about 1890).

number of families who have lived in the village for generations are still alive and well and producing sons and grandsons and the names of Batt, Buss, Cooper, Cornes, Gurr, Judge, Morris, Offen and Ottaway are still cropping up again and again in village records. Some of my childhood friends, the grocer, the baker and the shoemaker have gone forever, but I hope they will always be remembered.

Wedding photo of Mr. Edgar King to Miss C. Underdown on November 19, 1902, at Gilletts. The Hinds children who lived at Gilletts are seated in the front.

Christmas shooting party in the early 1900s at Vesper Hawk Farm where Mr. "Diddle-Eye" Batt lived. The guns are all brothers. Back row: George, Charles, Dan, Jim, Eb, Harry and Mark Batt. Seated: Alfred, Edwin "Diddle-Eye", Will. They were shooting blackbirds, jays and magpies.
(Mr. Harry Batt)

Smarden football team in the 1890s. Standing, left to right: Mr. Morley, Ben Springett, H. Stevens, G. Pearson, G. Buckman, J. Pearson, J. Butler. Seated: A. Anes, W. Burton, Mr. Martin (Schoolmaster), F. Pearson, H. Heathfield. (Photo lent by Mrs. Albert Collison)

Young girls' Springtime gym display on the Minnis, in the early 1930s.

SMARDEN'S CHILDREN

Mr. Chivers was our milkman for many years and his donkey and cart were a great attraction to all Smarden children. This was taken in 1962, on Smarden Street in front of the wood factory.

May Millen Marshall, Captain of the Smarden Hockey Club, and her little niece. Taken in 1920. (Mrs. S. Batt)

Gymkhanas are a common event in Smarden and children start riding ponies and competing in events at a very early age.

39

With the go-cart: Frank, Venetia and James Morris in 1895. Photo lent by Mrs. R. Sorrell, daughter of Venetia.

Lizzie Millen, pictured here aged 4, in 1900 when living at Snap Mill.
(Mrs. E. Ledger)

Vina Munn, aged 5 years, who lived at White Cottage in 1918.

Town Pond with Waterside House in the background. This picture was taken during the winter of 1963 when we all skated on the thick ice.

PONDS

Every large house in Smarden has a pond nearby. Our cottages, Wistaria cottage next door, the Chequers Inn as well as Gillet's Farmhouse opposite were all built around Town Pond. Until 1850 it was the only water supply for many households and was known as "the dipping". At that time it was square, with clean banks, clear of weeds and only small fish lived in it.

Halford L. Mills writes in his book about the River Beult and Ponds of the Weald in 1930 that in his childhood it was the reservoir for the supply of about twenty houses and five stables.

"A rough square of 30 rods of clean surface with a few yellow lilies, not cumbered with flags or bull-rushes, the banks not much overhung with willow or quinces."

There were four well-fenced dippings at the south side. Halford Mills writes that he was sent daily to "the dipping" as soon as he was old enough to fetch his load, with a small yoke and pails.

Today Town Pond is part of our garden which we share with our neighbours. It has a spring in the middle, said to be 14 feet deep but during the winter of 1963 it was so cold for so long that we actually lit a bonfire in the centre of the pond and the ice did not crack for nearly eight weeks.

Everyone comes to Water Lane when the flood waters rise. Nov. 1962.

This was our first big flood when the pond in our garden met the road. My mother almost enjoyed that one, but I was already a bit sceptical. Nov. 1960.

Water Lane always gets flooded at least once a year when the River Beult overflows its banks. The children like riding through the water on their bicycles. Nov. 1962.

My brothers paddling down Water Lane after our big flood in 1979. They operated a ferry service from the Chequers pub to Hartnup corner.

FLOODS

The River Beult decides to flood suddenly once or twice a year and when it does, the residents of Water Lane must take rapid precautions. Often our pond overflows into the road and Waterside House becomes an island. We have baffle boards and sand bags ready to lay down at the first sign of the river overflowing our way. The water entered our house only once, causing extensive damage. It was an experience to remember.

I was returning from a party but there was no one to meet me at the station. "Sorry," they said when I rang home. "We can't come. There's a river outside the door. You'll have to walk."

I got a lift with an old man who lived around the corner from us. Little did we know what was in store. As we neared Hadman's Bridge we saw that the river Beult had overflowed her banks and flooded over the bridge itself. Fields on either side were submerged in water and cows and sheep left stranded on the banks. A lorry was trying desperately to cross the bridge but the water was well over the wheels and it was impossible to move either forwards or backwards.

"I think we'd better try Town Bridge", the old man said, but that was no better. The flood waters were just as high and we couldn't wade as we were already up to our knees in the water, which was extremely cold.

Finally I managed to find a telephone and I called my family to the rescue. My brothers appeared twenty minutes later with a large pair of wellingtons and a wooden boat so I jumped in and we rowed home. Our house was totally surrounded by muddy water.

Inside everyone was dashing around with buckets and mops and our oak parquet flooring that my father had laid himself was cracked and warped and floating around like a lot of corn flakes in a foot of smelly water.

It was sad to see the damage made by the flood but there was no time to lament for as soon as the level went down inside the house a band of hefty men brought in an enormous hot air blower to try to dry things out while Jonny and Peter were busy outside with the boat operating a ferry service from the Chequers pub to Hartnup corner.

Since then the River Board and the County Council have dredged and cleared the Beult so that it now only comes lapping up to our kitchen doorstep. We have an early warning system amongst our neighbours and when there is a slight possibility of flood danger, the police ring our two local flood wardens. The alert goes quickly from house to house and it is all hands to the baffle boards.

SEASONS

"To every thing there is a season".

Spring: It seems to come a bit late each year — but the daffodils and primroses we planted years ago come up without fail, and multiply.

Summer: Water lilies in our pond and long lazy days in the sun.

Autumn: Leaves have fallen off the lime trees on Water Lane, giving a better view of Water Lane. Tombstones in the Churchyard with weathered inscriptions in the foreground.

Winter: The joys of winter — frost on the windowpane, snow crunching underfoot, and Smarden like a scene from Dickens.

Icicles on our windows in January.

Smarden soccer team on the Minnis. In the background is the village school.

THE MINNIS

The village green in the centre of Smarden has been called The Minnis from time immemorial. Minnis comes from the old Kent word "Mennys" meaning a high common or waste piece of rising ground. But no ground is wasted in the Smarden Minnis and it is used by young and old for all kinds of sport. There are football and rugger fields, tennis courts and playgrounds for the children. Village events usually take place on the Minnis with Guy Fawkes Bonfire night being an annual event and drawing larger crowds each year.

TRAFFIC

It wasn't until the motor car appeared on our small roads that Smarden began to change from a little self-contained community into a country village in close contact with the rest of the world. The 20th Century with its overwhelming social changes and the effects of the machine age transformed everything and everyone.

Gradually the weight of traffic built up until recently a new hazard arose when truck drivers realised that Smarden, on the map, is a short-cut from the port of Dover to many industrial sites in the southeast of England. Huge lorries and juggernauts suddenly started charging through narrow streets and tight bends and the chaos and confusion that followed took a great deal of sorting out. Some trucks could, with careful manoeuvring, backing up and edging slowly forward, manage to get around the very tight corner by the Chequers Inn at the top of The Street. But the huge juggernauts and largest lorries could not. Result: hour-long traffic jams and extensive old-world damage. These pictures describe the problem. The Chequers' unique rounded weatherboarding was damaged time and time again. Brown's shop windows were cracked and broken.

A tight situation as a large lorry squeezes through the narrow road leading past the Chequers Inn into the Street. The Chequers' ancient and unique curved weatherboarding has recently been repainted.

The former Buckles Bakery was hit and the sisters Harriet, whose ancient cottage heads The Street, had bricks and tiles knocked off at least once a month. After many such incidents, special town meetings were called and the police, traffic experts and Ashford Borough councillors summoned. A plan of action was devised. Smarden itself was re-routed with all heavy traffic to make a detour around the village. But in spite of large signs and new maps, we still get huge juggernauts caught in our midst. The drivers, and one has to feel somewhat sorry for them, are usually French, Spanish, German or Turkish and interpreters are often needed.

A car carrier tries to turn into Cage Lane at the top of The Street. House-owners hold their breath.

A large lorry tries to manoeuvre around the bend from Water Lane into the Street.

The crooked house, owned by the Weeks brothers.

THE CROOKED HOUSE

Of all the beautiful houses in Smarden, I have always loved this tumble-down cottage owned by the Weeks brothers who have lived here for generations. One of the Weeks brothers was the local barber. When I was a little girl I used to watch him from the road as he cut the hair of the local farmers — straight back and sides — in his open-air salon. The gingerbread look of the house, which has no "mod cons" or indeed electricity, has a cosy, weathered appeal which no modern bungalow could ever capture and I delight in showing it off to my friends as my favourite house in Smarden.

Perhaps one day my favourite house will tumble down, or an adventurous soul with an artistic eye might convert it into a more liveable home as my father converted "Doctor's Cottages" a quarter of a century ago.

But for now I'm proud that it is a part of Smarden's heritage, with its wavy roof and peeling weatherboard and its old thatched barn.

The Weeks brothers' hair-cutting salon in front of their thatched barn.